At Be The Future, it's important to us that our products have as little impact on the planet as possible and use cyclical processes.

We're on a mission to help people like you who care about the planet to educate friends, families, grandparents, cousins and neighbours about how we can help the planet.

Ideally, we would love to print this book in a fully sustainable way, however, the book industry is not there yet and to print it independently would make the book unaffordable. In response to this challenge and in order to reduce production and consumption, we have designed this book with the intention that you will loan it, pass it on, share it, gift it, and most of all, love it.

Help the book to tell its own story of how it has been passed on through families, friends and generations. On the next page, fill in the bubbles, create your own bubbles, write notes to the next person, stick things in, do a doodle.

We hope you enjoy it as much as we have enjoyed creating it for you.

Sally & Helen

This book first belonged to:

who passed it onto:

& loaned it to:

who read it with:

who gave it to:

Copyright ©BeTheFuture
Published 2024

The right of Sally Giblin and Helen Hill of Be The Future to be identified as author of this Work has been asserted by them in accordance with sections 77 and 78 of the Copyright, Designs and Patents Act 1988.
All rights reserved.

No part of this publication may be reproduced, stored in a retrieval system, copied in any form or by any means (electronic, mechanical, photocopying, recording or otherwise) without the prior written permission from the publisher.

Requests for permission should be sent to Be The Future via hello@bethefuture.earth
A CIP catalogue record for this book is available from the British Library.

ISBN 978-1-9196385-3-9 (paperback)
ISBN 978-1-9196385-4-6 (hardback)

Written by Sally Giblin
Edited by Brooke Vitale
Illustrated by Helen Hill

The day the Crab got Crabby

Sally Giblin

Illustrated by
Helen Hill

Crab laughed.

"Well, I love it as much as parrotfish love to make sand with their fish-plops!"

ewwwww gross

"I do NO such thing!"

purrrrrrp

<ahem>

"Something smells fishy," muttered Crab. "I've never seen such a big boat on the reef."

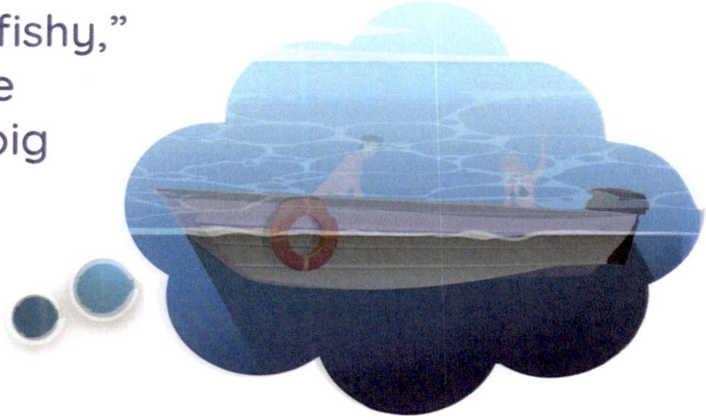

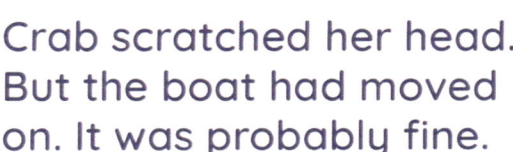

Crab scratched her head. But the boat had moved on. It was probably fine.

"Come on, let's go climb coral!" said Crab. So Crab and Sea Anemone

crawled and **climbed**, **STRETCHED** and *strained*.

But before they could reach the top of the coral ...

"Are you okay?"
asked Crab.

"I'm fine, I'm just a little sore.
It's the coral reef I worry for."

"We have to fix this plastic soup!
We need more friends to join our group!"

And with that, Sea Anemone grew from

one to two

Crab and the Sea Anemones darted across the water until they came across Dolphin and her calf resting on a bed of sponge.

"Dolphin," worried Crab, "we're in a pinch! A jumble of plastic is

tumbling

onto our reef. The plastic will smother it. Can you help us stop the plastic soup?"

"There's plastic all over the ocean," Dolphin replied. "The problem is too big for us to fix. So why bother? Come relaaaax with us."

insisted Crab, and she and the Sea Anemones hurried on.

As they clambered through the coral reef, the Sea Anemones were KNOCKED over again by a plastic pen!

"We have to fix this plastic soup!
We need more friends to join our group!"

the Sea Anemones rapped.

And with that, the Sea Anemones grew from

two to four

POP

POP

help, I'm seeing double!

"Shark," pleaded Crab, "we're in hot water! A hodgepodge of plastic is raining onto our reef.

What if your pups mistake it for food? Can you help us stop the plastic soup?"

"I hope you can, Shark. You've got your fins full here! We'll find someone else to help," insisted Crab.

She and the Sea Anemones rushed on.

Once again the Sea Anemones rapped,

"We have to fix this plastic soup!
We need more friends to join our group!"

And with that, the Sea Anemones grew from

four to eight.

Dashing along, Crab and the Sea Anemones noticed Parrotfish nibbling on the coral.

"Parrotfish!" Crab cried. "There's plastic raining onto the reef and no one's willing to help! I'm getting crabby! The plastic will make the reef sick! Can you help?"

mmm-mmm tastyyyy

"Eh, how much damage can a bit of plastic do?" shrugged Parrotfish.

"All I need is algae to eat and I'm happy."

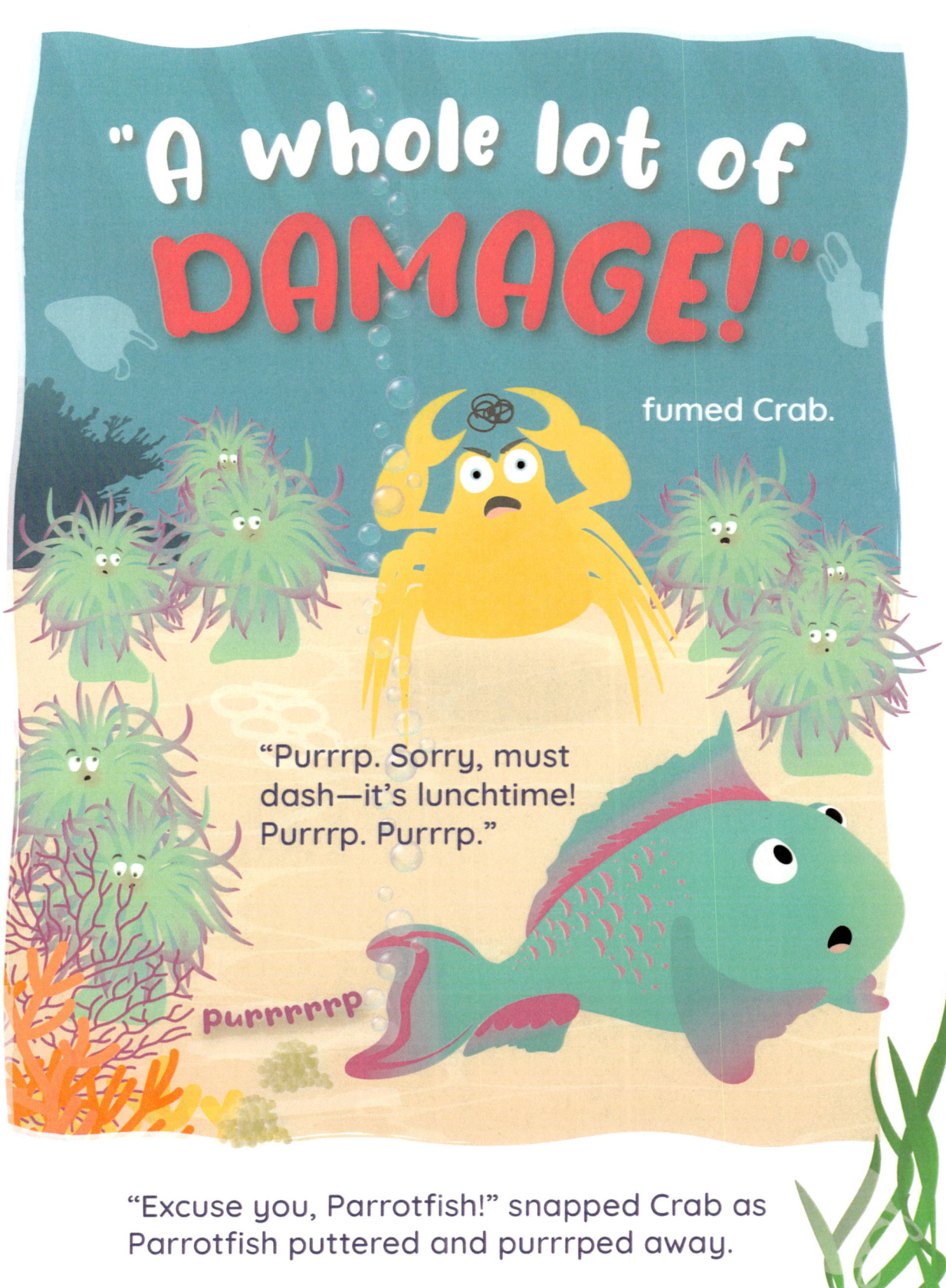

"The coral must be saved, but how? We have to make them listen now!" cried the Sea Anemones.

And they shimmied and they shook until **eight** became **sixteen**.

Then they quivered and they quaked until **sixteen** became **thirty two**.

They multiplied over and over until the reef became a carpet of **swaying** Sea Anemones.

it's a takeover!

At that moment, Crab and the Sea Anemones heard a cry …

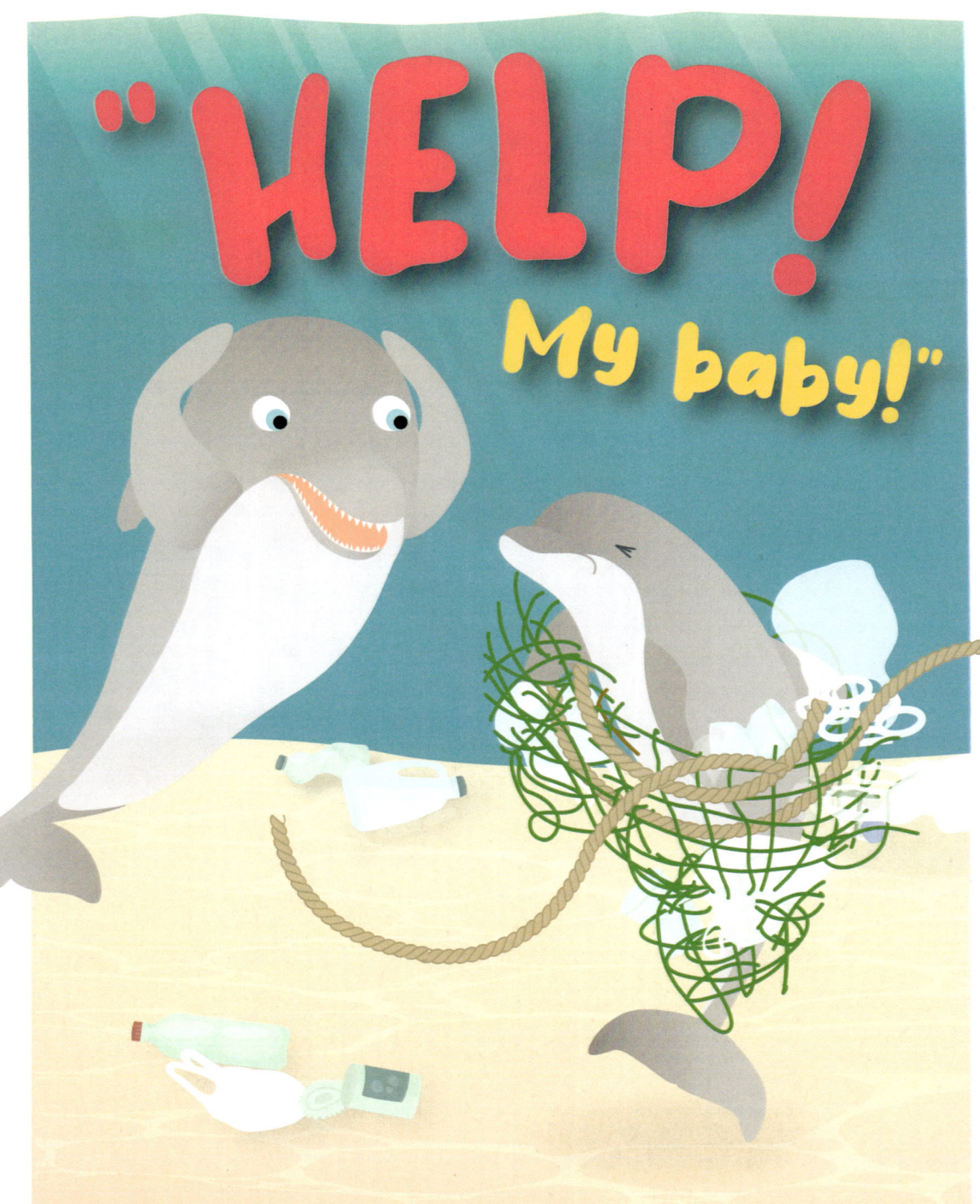

It was Dolphin! Her baby was tangled in a twirl of plastic cups and a swirl of plastic bags.
"We have to do something!" cried Crab.

With that, the colony of Sea Anemones chorused:

"Young Dolphin's stuck in plastic soup!
He needs your help! Come join our group."

The sea creatures sped over to help.

They PUSHED and pulled,
they lifted and shifted,
they JOLTED and jerked ...

... and POP

Little Dolphin swam free!

The sea creatures flapped their fins and twitched their tentacles.

Crab thought for a moment.
Then she declared,

We need the humans to join our group! But how?

As the sea creatures pondered and purrrped and planned, the sun found its way between the swirling plastic to their rainbow reef.

Crab turned to the Sea Anemones and **gasped**,

"Let's go show more humans!"

Crab cried as they flipped, spinned and swam to the next beach.

-giddy up Sharkface!-

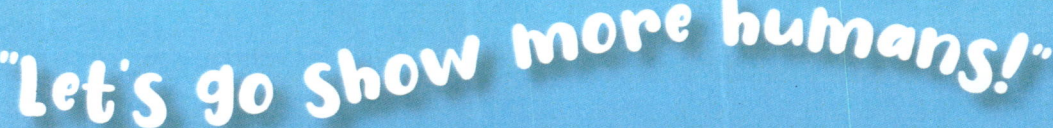

www.ingramcontent.com/pod-product-compliance
Lightning Source LLC
Chambersburg PA
CBRC100224100526
44590CB00009B/150